For Zio Simone,
who makes the best X-rays.

Fox has a box, and in his box he has a...

Xylophone.

Fox has a box, and in his box he has an...

X-ray.

Fox has a box, and in his box he has a...

number six.

Fox has a box, and in his box he has an...

axe.

Fox has a box, and in his box he has...

an X.

Fox has a box, and in his box he has...

Texas.

Fox has a box, and in his box he has...

phlox.

Fox has a box, and in his box he has...

beeswax.

Now, Fox has... an empty box.

X Words

fox

box

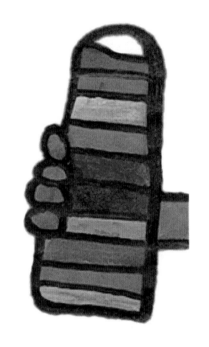

xylophone

phlox

six

Texas

x-ray fish

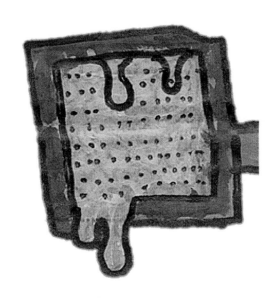

beeswax

axe

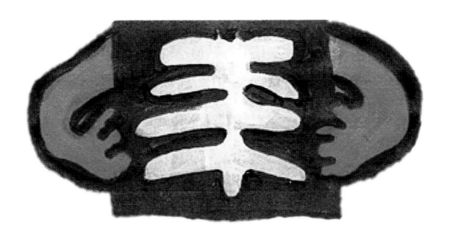

X-ray

X is for Box Art!

BOX Art
is painting
or drawing a
picture onto
a box.

X is for Box Art

Make your own BOX Art, by finding a cardboard box and using paints and markers to draw a picture!

Fox has a box, and in his box he has a six.

AlphaBOX Book Series

APPLES AND APRICOTS
by H.P. Gentileschi
A

Boy on a Bus
by H.P. Gentileschi
B

Cat in a Cup
by H.P. Gentileschi
C

Duck's Days
by H.P. Gentileschi
D

Elephant's Easter Eggs
by H.P. Gentileschi
E

Is This a Fish?
by H.P. Gentileschi
F

Gorillas Like Gum
by H.P. Gentileschi
G

THIS HAND
by H.P. Gentileschi
H

INSECTS in my ICE-CREAM
by H.P. Gentileschi
I

When Do You Drink Juice?
by H.P. Gentileschi
J

WHERE IS KATE'S KEY?
by H.P. Gentileschi
K

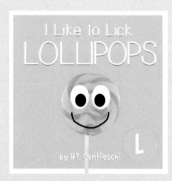

I Like to Lick LOLLIPOPS
by H.P. Gentileschi
L

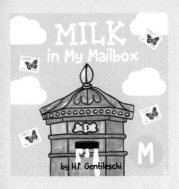

MILK in My Mailbox
by H.P. Gentileschi
M

DOES A NUT HAVE A NOSE?
by H.P. Gentileschi
N

ONE OCTOPUS in the Olive Tree
by H.P. Gentileschi
O

penguin's paper plane
by H.P. Gentileschi
P

The Queen's Question
by H.P. Gentileschi
Q

Rabbit's Rainbow in Rome
by H.P. Gentileschi
R

Snake's Snacks
by H.P. Gentileschi
S

Does a Tomato Have Teeth?
by H.P. Gentileschi
T

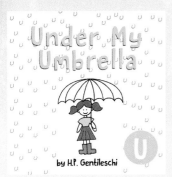

Under My Umbrella
by H.P. Gentileschi
U

Victoria's Violin
by H.P. Gentileschi
V

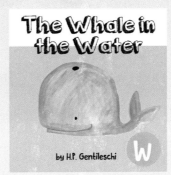

The Whale in the Water
by H.P. Gentileschi
W

Fox Has A Box
by H.P. Gentileschi
X

YOUR YELLOW YO-YO
by H.P. Gentileschi
Y

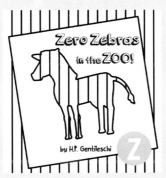

Zero Zebras in the ZOO!
by H.P. Gentileschi
Z

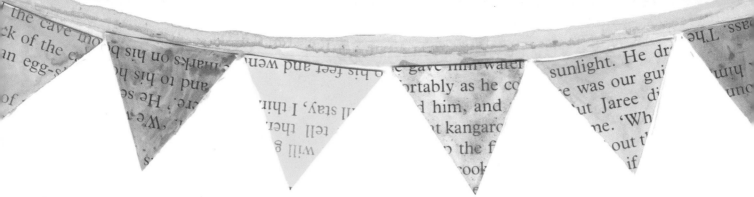

For more engaging activities, teaching resources and to learn more about AlphaBOX books, follow H.P. Gentileschi on:

H.P. Gentileschi

www.hpgentileschi.com

hpgentileschi@gmail.com

We'd love to see how you're using the AlphaBOX series!
Share and tag your photos using:
#alphaboxbooks

Made in the USA
Monee, IL
17 March 2023

30071240R00017